COOKING
IN THE GREAT
OUTDOORS

By Earl Shelsby

Phoenix, Md.

**Distributed exclusively to the book trade by
Stackpole Books
Cameron & Kelker Streets
P.O. Box 1831
Harrisburg, PA 17105
1-800-732-3669**

Published by FIM Publishing, Inc.
P.O. Box 197, Phoenix, MD 21131

Printed in the United States of America

Pocket Guide Series
ISBN   0-917131-00-2

Cooking in the Great Outdoors
ISBN   0-917131-04-5

To our national leaders and outdoor organizations who were smart enough to save a bit of our national treasure, the great outdoors, for us and future generations to enjoy. Keep up the good work.

CONTENTS

Planning The Menu

Just as camp cooking has changed, so has camping. It's important that you figure the limitations of where you will be camping into the menu you plan.

Have The Right Gear

The basic rule is match the amount of gear you take to the transportation to and from camp. If you have to carry it on your back, you'll really want to limit it.

Breakfast

A little planning can really get you off to a good day in the field or on the water with a first class breakfast.

Lunch

Depending on your situation, you will find these recipes adequate for a light dinner, as well.

Dinner

Not only are these recipes great when camping, but at home as well when you want a quick, tasty dish

Fish & Game

If you're fishing or hunting, here are some recipes you'll love.

Preparing Fish

Planning Index
(Review First)

Planning The Menu

Camp cooking isn't what it used to be, but camping has changed a lot, too. Some camps today have all the conveniences of home including electricity, microwaves, ranges, refrigeration and many of the labor-saving kitchen devices. Also, backpacking into the most remote parts of the outdoors where none of the kitchen amenities are available is extremely popular. Most camps fall somewhere in between these two extremes.

Wherever your camp falls in this range, there is the common ground that you need to feed the campers well without enslaving one person with cooking duties while others are enjoying the hunting, fishing or just communicating with nature. We will deal mostly with the more primitive camp cooking, but there is some good advice for the outdoorsmen who have the more plush camps.

Not everyone is a natural cook, but you don't have to be to produce meals that are not only palatable, but easy as boiling water and not much more time consuming.

The first step in satisfying hungry outdoorsmen is to plan your meals for the duration of the stay. Every meal should be planned in detail to include every ingredient. In the wilderness it is very unlikely that the opportunity of a last minute dash to the supermarket is available.

A few years back, I camped on an island in the Caribbean for six days. There was nothing on the island but sand, grass and palm trees. There was no fresh water. However, the fishing opportunities were great. The island was 90 air miles from Key West, but that didn't matter because the float plane pilot dropped my partner and me off and did not return until he was scheduled to pick us up on the sixth day. This is the ultimate case of "if you forget it, you do without it."

We had made arrangements for a boat, tent, cooking gear and gasoline to be delivered to the island by a fishing boat. Because of the lack of space on the float plane we were limited to one ice chest, five gallons of water, fishing equipment, and one small backpack each.

Meats and some vegetables for all six days were frozen and put in the ice chest and covered with ice. Eggs, bacon and a limited number of canned beverages were stored on top the ice. Canned vegetables to complete the menu and snacks were stored in the backpacks.

The camp rule was established that the ice chest was to be opened twice a day. Once in the morning to dig the foods of the day out of the ice and remove foods for breakfast and lunch. The second opening of the ice chest was in the evening for beverages and the food for the evening meal.

The reason for this strict rule was to conserve the ice which was not replaceable on the island. Despite daily temperatures in the high 90's and very little shade, there was considerable ice and some partially frozen food in the chest when we were picked up.

I have had a wilderness experience where cooking was a real chore. I was flown into a spike camp in the Brooks Range of Alaska with three other hunters. The outfitter and pilot had planned to make three trips to the camp, but the third flight was canceled because of heavy snow. Of course, the food was scheduled to be delivered on that third trip.

Heavy fog and snow kept the bush plane grounded for seven days. Fortunately, the camp was on a stream that was full of grayling and we had emergency rations of freeze dried noodles and candy bars in our backpacks. If there is an experience that can make you appreciate a well planned camp menu, it is eating freeze dried noodles and grayling three times a day for six straight days. The last day we were there, we had the welcome change of pan-fried Doll sheep and freeze dried noodles. One of the hunters walked up on a sheep in the fog.

Consider the limitations of your campsite or possibly several sites when planning the menu. If there is no water available, consider meals that can be made with the amount of water you can transport to the site. You might consider canned foods because they contain water, but are a lot heavier to tote to camp.

Another limitation could be whether you can build a campfire. Campfires are prohibited in some wilderness areas, particularly during droughts. If you have to tote in a one-burner stove, you might want to plan as many one-pot meals as possible.

Lack of refrigeration is also a limitation that must be considered. If you can drive your four-wheeler to the campsite, an ice chest solves the problem for two or three days. You can stretch it out to a week like I did on the island. But if your campsite can only be reached by hiking several miles over rough terrain, you will want light (in weight) and non-perishable foods like freeze dried meals.

Once you have your menu planned, that includes backups for those days when the fish don't bite or the weather prevents fishing, you should do as much of the prep work as possible before leaving home. Mix spices, chop vegetables, cut meats and seal them in containers or zip-locked plastics. Besides being a lot more comfortable to do in a kitchen, it cuts down on the time needed to cook in camp.

Plan one-pot meals as often as possible, even if you have facilities, because of ease and quickness. Besides, the fewer pots you use, the less time you will spend washing pots and pans and the more time you will have for fun. Asian stir fries are easy and quick and can be done in a frying pan as well as a wok. Mexican dishes, many of which were derived from the camp cooking of the American Indians, add zip to camp meals and can be easy and quick to make. Stews and meat-vegetable combinations are good choices.

Utilize herbs and spices to put zest into your camp meals. Too many American cooks think the only seasonings are salt and pepper. I agree that salt and pepper are great, but sprinkle a little rosemary or basil on a boiled potato after you have put salt and pepper on it and you have a different taste. Try it. You might like it. Onions and garlic are also under utilized by a lot of cooks. I've been accused of putting onion and/or garlic in everything but my tea. It's not true. I don't drink tea and I almost never put either in my desserts.

Another great seasoner is cheese. Vegetables, meats, and fish can be made more palatable with the addition of one of the many great cheeses of the world. Use them in your camp meals when it is practical.

Portable camp stoves are made with one to three burners and are fueled by either propane or unleaded gas. The more remote the camp, the smaller the stove. In the wild, you will most likely be using a one burner or a campfire. If you have a choice, use the one-burner propane stove. Campfires are a last resort for cooking because the heat is difficult to control and the tar that collects on the outside of pots is not easy to clean in the wilderness.

Bread is often a problem for campers. A loaf of bread is bulky to carry and will usually go stale in about three days. My answer to this is tortillas, the basic Mexican or Indian bread. A little flour or cornmeal, lard or margarine, baking powder, salt and water can be mixed and baked in an ungreased frying pan over medium heat. A recipe for tortillas will be included in the lunch recipe section.

A cutting board is essential to cooking. However, when camping in remote areas it is an item you may try to do without. That may not be a wise decision, but some substitutes are a flat rock, a tree stump or a canoe or boat oar. If you want to fillet a fish or roll dough for tortillas, they can save the day.

As stated before, campfires are not the greatest way to cook because of the difficulty of controlling heat. But in a really primitive area, a campfire is the only way you have of baking foods. Pioneers and Indians used to bake foods by sealing them in clay. In these modern days aluminum foil serves the same purpose and it is a lot easier to use.

The trick in baking in the coals of a campfire is to allow it to die down to a bed of coals, which is constant heat. Put your foil wrapped meal in the coals, but check it frequently or you may have charcoal for dinner.

As mentioned earlier, if you didn't bring it with you, chances are you will have to do without it. Thus, the outdoorsman who plans carefully is better off.

Have The Right Gear

The basic rule is take all that you can carry with the transportation being used. Canoes and small boats can be limiting. The same for walking.

Because of the inefficiency of campfires and no-fire policies in some wilderness areas, a camp stove is a must. They start with the propane one-burners designed for back-packers. They fold up into a size that fits into a back-pack and one propane tank will usually last a week. Two and three bur-ner camp stoves take up more space and weight, but the extra burners are a

Camp stoves come in one to three burner mod-els. If you have space, two burner models are great.

special luxury if your transportation will carry them.

In pots and pans, the minimum requirement is a pot big enough to fix a meal for all in camp, a frying pan, covers for both the pot and the frying pan, a plastic mixing bowl with cover, a knife, fork and spoon for everyone, a tablespoon, a good sharp knife,

A single burner stove is best suited to more primitive areas.

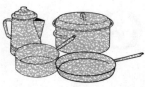

This much equipment, in the pot and pan category, is nice to have if your situation allows for it.

a spatula and a plate for each person. If you are camping alone, you can eliminate the plate because you can eat right out of the pot or pan. If space allows, a second pot is a wise choice because it is available for side dishes and making warm beverages.

There are some really compact kits on the market that contain most of these essentials. They are light weight because the are designed for backpackers.

Last, but not least, is water-proofed matches. You can make them yourself by dipping wooden matches into melted paraffin. I've spent a lot of time in the wilderness, but I've never learned to make a fire with flint and steel or rubbing sticks together. A cold camp without a fire is a miserable camp, especially when you are hungry.

Another thing I like to take to camp with me is a ready cooked meal, like a pot of chili or stew, if possible. The first evening in camp can be hectic. If you have a meal that can be ready by just heating, it might be just the relief you need on that first evening in camp.

Breakfast

Special French Toast

French toast is a great way to start the day in camp, particularly if there are youngsters with you. This one can be started on the night before and tossed in the frying pan and ready in a few minutes.

It can be done even farther ahead at home, putting the seasoned bread in zip-lock bags making breakfast a snap. They should be kept on ice until ready to use.

This, as the title indicates, is not the ordinary French toast.

Ingredients:
2 eggs
3 oz milk
1 tsp grated orange peel
1 tsp ground cinnamon
2 oz orange juice
1 tbs sugar
1 tps vanilla
4 thick slices French bread

Directions:

In bowl combine eggs, orange juice, milk, sugar, orange peel, vanilla, and cinnamon. Beat until well mixed. You can use a blender if preparing at home before the camping trip. Arrange bread slices in single layer in shallow dish pour egg mixture over bread. Turn several times to coat well. Cover with saran wrap and refrigerate overnight. Pan fry in corn oil margarine or butter. Sprinkle with confectioners sugar; if desired serve with syrup.

Bermuda Johnny Bread

Something a little different for breakfast always adds to the enjoyment of camp. This can be made up ahead of time, put in a zip-locked bag and kept on ice for a day or two before cooking.

Ingredients:
¼ cup sugar
¼ tsp salt
1 egg
2 tbs butter
1½ cup flour
2 tsp baking powder
½ cup milk

Directions:
Mix sugar, flour, salt, and baking powder. Add egg and milk and mix. Melt butter in frying pan. Spoon a third of the batter into the pan. Fry on low heat until brown. Turn and brown the otherside. Repeat twice with the remaining batter. Split bread in half and serve with plenty of butter and jam.

Potato Omelette

This is a takeoff on a Spanish appetizer, but it makes a great breakfast in camp or at home.

Ingredients:
2 potatoes, boiled, diced
1 can mushrooms, drained
salt & pepper to taste
3 eggs
1 oz shredded cheddar cheese
vegetable oil

Directions:
Beat the eggs lightly and add diced potato, mushroom pieces and cheese. (Add anything you like, really. If you wish to chop and saute some onion and bell pepper to add, that would be delicious too.) Pour into heated frying pan with oil and fry over medium heat until egg is solid. Season to your liking and carefully fold out onto a plate.

Baconed Hominy

This Seminole Indian breakfast is a good way to start a day in camp.

Ingredients:
8 strips bacon, in small pieces
salt and pepper to taste
1 large can hominy
3 scallions, chopped

Directions:
Fry the bacon pieces in a large skillet until well browned and crisp. Add the hominy, salt and pepper and cook stirring continuously for 6-7 minutes. Add scallions and continue cooking for an additional 5 minutes. Serve immediately.

SPECKKARTOFFEL (Potatoes with Bacon)

Toting sour cream to camp is a bother most of the time, but this breakfast my German grandmother used to make for me makes it difficult for me to go camping without it.

Ingredients
¼ lb bacon, cubed
1 tbs lard
salt to taste
1 lb potatoes, cooked, sliced
4 - 5 tbs sour cream
pepper to taste

Directions:
In a skillet, melt the lard and briefly fry the onions and bacon. Add the sliced potatoes and saute until golden brown. Add salt and pepper to taste, and mix in the sour cream.

Basque Shepherd's Pie

This delightful breakfast isn't as difficult as it looks.

Ingredients:
4 slices bacon
2 tsp sliced green onions/tops
¾ tsp salt
1 dash pepper
3 med. potatoes
1 tbs snipped parsley
⅛ tsp dried thyme, crushed
4 large eggs

Directions:

In skillet cook bacon until crisp; drain, reserving 2 tbs of drippings. Crumble bacon and set aside. In same skillet combine reserved drippings, peeled, thinly sliced potatoes, onion, parsley, salt, thyme and pepper. Cover tightly; cook over low heat till potatoes are barely tender, 20 to 25 minutes, stirring carefully once or twice. In small bowl beat together eggs and milk; pour over potato mixture. Cover and continue cooking over very low heat till egg is set in center, 8 to 10 minutes.

With a wide spatula, loosen sides and bottom and slide potatoes out onto serving plate, or serve from skillet. Sprinkle crumbled bacon atop. Serve hot.

Mexican-Style Scrambled Eggs

Add some jalapeno peppers to this concoction for a really zesty breakfast

Ingredients:
4 flour tortillas*
¼ cup water
2 tbs taco sauce
dash of pepper
¾ cup taco sauce, divided
4 eggs
2 tbs chopped canned green chilies
¼ tsp salt
1 tbs vegetable cooking spray
½ cup + 1 tbs cheddar, shredded

Directions:
Combine eggs, water, chilies, 2 tbs taco sauce, salt and pepper in a bowl; mix well. Pour egg mixture into a skillet coated with cooking spray; cook over medium heat, stirring often, until eggs are firm but still moist. Spoon one-forth of the egg mixture onto each tortilla. Top with 1 tablespoon taco sauce and 1 tablespoon cheese; fold opposite sides over. Garnish each tortilla with 1 tablespoon taco sauce and 1/2 tablespoon cheese.

* See page 26 for recipe.

Tara Pork Scramble

A Southern style breakfast.

Ingredients:
2 slices salt pork
1 (12 oz) can whole kernel corn
dash of pepper
4 eggs, slightly beaten
1 cup milk

Directions:

Dice salt pork and fry until brown; pour off all but 3 tbs of the fat. Add mixture of egg, corn, milk, and pepper to pork frying. Add salt if needed. Cook over low heat, stirring constantly until set.

Apple Omelette

Ingredients:
2½ tbs all purpose flour
½ cup milk
4 tsp sugar
2 apples, peeled and thinly sliced
pinch salt
2 eggs, beaten
1 grated lemon rind
1 - 3 tbs unsalted butter

Directions:

Make a thin, smooth batter with the flour, milk and salt. Add the beaten eggs, sugar and lemon rind and beat well. Gently stir the apple slices into the batter. Melt some butter in an 8 inch frying pan. Pour in the apple mixture making sure to distribute the apple slices evenly over the bottom of the pan. Cook over a medium heat until the omelette is set and golden brown on the bottom. Then, using whatever technique works for you, turn the omelette over and brown the other side. When done, slide the omelette onto a heated plate, sprinkle with confectioner's sugar and serve.

Special Potato Frittata

Here is a breakfast better than many get at home. With the cheese and seasonings, it makes getting up in the morning a pleasure.

Ingredients:
¼ stick butter
2 tbs olive oil
3 potatoes, diced
¼ cup grated parmesan
¾ tsp paprika
¼ tsp garlic powder
⅛ tsp Italian seasoning
4 eggs, beaten to blend
2 tbs all purpose flour
salt and ground pepper

Directions:
Melt butter with oil in skillet over medium heat. Mix potatoes and flour. Add potato, paprika, garlic powder and Italian seasoning to skillet and cook until potatoes are just tender, stirring often for 10 minutes. Combine eggs with parmesan cheese in medium bowl. Season with salt and pepper. Pour egg mixture over potatoes. Pierce holes in egg mixture and lift edges with spatula, tipping pan to allow uncooked egg to flow under, until edge forms, about one minute; do not stir. Reduce heat to low, cover skillet and continue until eggs are set.

Peanut Butter French Toast

Another variation of French toast that will help make happy campers.

Ingredients:
½ cup peanut butter
4 slices white bread
¼ tsp salt

½ cup milk
1/3 cup applesauce
2 eggs
1½ tsp sugar

Directions:

Mix peanut butter and applesauce. Spread mixture on 2 slices white bread. Top with remaining bread slices.

Beat eggs, slightly. Add salt, sugar, and milk. Mix well. Dip sandwiches in this egg mixture and fry in butter.

Chili Omelet with Rice

Here is a zesty breakfast that can be made with either frying pan or wok in a few minutes.

Ingredients:
4 eggs
1 tsp chili powder
⅛ tsp pepper
½ green bell pepper, chopped
½ cup cold cooked rice
½ tsp salt
¼ cup chopped onion
1 tbs butter

Directions:

In a medium bowl, beat eggs and egg whites until blended; stir in rice, chili powder, salt and black pepper. Place frying pan or wok over high eat. When hot, add onion and bell pepper; stir-fry 1 minute or until crisp-tender.

Reduce heat to medium-low; add butter. When melted, pour in egg mixture; cook until set on bottom and sides. Gently lift cooked portion with spatula so that uncooked portion can flow to bottom. Cook until top is firm. Fold over and turn out onto warm plates.

Same Old Stuff (SOS)

Here is an old favorite for those who have served time in the military. Chipped beef can be substituted for the ground beef.

Ingredients:
½ lb ground beef
¼ cup flour
2 cups milk
1 diced onions
Salt, black pepper to taste

Directions:
In a frying pan, cook beef until it is no longer pink. Drain fat. Add onions and cook for about 3 minutes. Stir in flour, salt and pepper. Mix thoroughly and cook about 5 minutes or until flour is absorbed.

Stir in milk to cooked beef mixture. Heat to a simmer, stirring frequently. Cook until thickened. Serve hot over toast or biscuits.

Fried Apples

This might not make a complete breakfast for the hearty eaters, but it is a good start and a couple fried eggs could make up the deficiency. Make a lot because it makes a good side dish for the evening pork meal.

Ingredients:
6 large unpared, cored red apples
½ cup cooking wine
1 cup sugar
6″ cinnamon stick
3 tsp butter
½ cup water
1 tsp lemon juice

Directions:
Saute apples in butter for 6-8 minutes. Boil wine, sugar, cinnamon stick, and lemon juice for 5 minutes. Pour over apples. Cook, uncovered, until apples are tender. Pour into serving dish. Serve warm or cold.

Lunch

Flour Tortillas

Bread and rolls are difficult to transport when hiking because they are so crushable. However, tortillas are an easy-to-make substitute. The dough can be made up in advance and put in a zip-locked bag. Then you just fry up what you need as you need them. Rolling pins are a little bulky to carry. I usually use a beverage can or bottle to roll out my tortillas.

They are not hamburger rolls, but they will give a hamburger or any other sandwich a little different texture and taste.

Ingredients:
4 cups flour
⅛ tsp baking powder
1 cup plus 3 tbs hot water
2 tsp salt
2/3 cup shortening

Directions:

Combine flour, salt and baking powder, stirring well. Cut in shortening with a pastry blender until mixture resembles coarse meal. Gradually stir in water, mixing well. Shape dough into 1½ inch balls; roll each on a floured surface into a 6 inch circle. Cook tortillas in an ungreased skillet over medium heat about 2 minutes on each side or until lightly browned. Pat tortillas lightly with spatula while browning the second side if they puff during cooking. Yields 24 tortillas.

BBQ Tuna Burgers

Ingredients:
1 can (6½ ozs) solid white tuna
1 egg, slightly beaten
½ cup salad dressing
lettuce leaves
tomato slices
1 cup dry bread crumbs
½ cup minced celery
¼ cup finely chopped green onions
4 hamburger buns (or tortillas)

Directions:
Mash tuna with a fork. Mix in bread crumbs, egg, celery, salad dressing and onion. Form into 4 patties. Barbecue or fry 3 to 4 minutes on each side until cooked through. Place patties on lettuce-lined buns, garnish with sliced tomatoes and additional salad dressing.

Fish Cakes

Ingredients:
1 lb canned salmon (with liquid)
2 tbsp milk
salt and pepper to taste
2 eggs
leftover mashed potatoes

Directions:
Mix all ingredients together and shape into patties. Dip cakes in a mixture of 2 eggs beaten with 2 tbsp of cold water. Coat with bread crumbs and cook in skillet until well browned and warmed all the way through.

Finger Sandwiches

Ingredients:
¼ cup softened butter
2 tbs chopped chives
6 slices white bread
3 oz crumbled roquefort cheese
½ cup chopped watercress

Directions:
   Combine butter, roquefort, chives, and watercress. Blend thoroughly. Trim crusts from bread. Spread cheese mixture on 3 slices; top with remaining slices. Cut each sandwich into thirds.

Chili-Corn Burgers

Ingredients:
½ lb lean ground beef
1 tsp minced garlic
15 oz can corn kernels and liquid
1 tbs chili powder (or to taste)
4 sandwich buns or tortillas
1 cup chopped onion
½ cup diced bell pepper
16 oz can tomatoes
¼ tsp ground black pepper

Directions:
   Coarsely chop the tomatoes, reserve the juice.
Brown meat in skillet over medium heat, drain off any fat. Add onion, garlic and peppers, saute for 5 minutes or until the onion and pepper are soft.
   Stir in the corn and liquid, tomatoes and liquid, chili powder, and black pepper. Simmer, uncovered, 10 minutes, or until most of the liquid has evaporated. Serve on buns or tortillas.

Rinderrouladen (Beef Rolls)

This also makes a good entry for dinner. I like to make them up at home and keep them iced down for the first lunch in camp or the second night dinner.

Ingredients:
2 sandwich or roll steaks
½ tsp salt
2 pickles; dill
1 onion; large, chopped
1½ cup beef broth; hot
½ bay leaf
2 tsp mustard; Dijon-style
¼ tsp pepper
2 bacon; strips
¼ cup vegetable oil
4 peppercorns
1 tsp cornstarch

Directions:
Pickles, salt pork or bacon should be cut into long thin strips. Lay steaks on a flat surface. Spread each with mustard; sprinkle with salt and pepper. Divide pickles, bacon, and onion among the steaks equally. Roll up steaks jelly-roll fashion; secure with toothpicks, or thread. Heat oil in a skillet, add the steak rolls, and brown well on all sides, about 15 minutes. Pour in hot beef broth, peppercorns, and bay leaf. Cover and simmer for 35 minutes. Remove beef rolls, discard peppercorns and bay leaves. Mix cornstarch with a small amount of cold water, stir into gravy and bring to a boil. Boil until gravy is thick and bubbly. Correct seasonings and serve separately.

Beef and Cabbage Joes

Instead of hamburger buns, try wrapping a tortilla around this mixture.

Ingredients:
½ lb ground beef
¼ cup thinly sliced celery
¼ cup chopped green pepper
¼ cup water
1 tbs prepared mustard
1 medium onion, chopped
1 cup shredded cabbage
1/3 cup catsup
¼ tsp salt
4 hamburger buns, split/toasted

Directions:
Cook and stir meat, onion and celery in large skillet until meat is brown.

Drain off fat. Stir in cabbage, green pepper, catsup, water, salt and mustard; heat to boiling, stirring occasionally. Reduce heat; cover and simmer until vegetables are tender, about 25 minutes. Spoon mixture onto bottom halves of buns; top with remaining halves.

Black Bean Chili with Rice

Canned black beans will serve the purpose if you don't want to be bothered with soaking and cooking beans in camp.

Ingredients:
1 lb ground beef
1 cup green pepper, diced
1 carrot, diced
2 cloves garlic, minced
¼ to ½ tsp ground red pepper
4 cups hot cooked rice
3 cups cooked black beans

1 onion, chopped
1 tbs chili powder
2 bay leaves
3 cup tomato juice

Directions:

Cook beef in saucepan over medium heat, stirring to crumble. Add all ingredients except rice. Bring to a boil, simmer uncovered 20 to 25 minutes. Remove bay leaves. Serve over hot rice.

Skilletburgers

You might skip the bread and blend this mixture with some cooked macaroni instead of making sandwiches.

Ingredients:

1 lb ground beef
1 green pepper, seeded
2 tbs sugar
1 tbs vinegar
4 hamburger buns (or tortillas)
1 large onion
¾ cup ketchup
2 tbs prepared mustard
½ tsp salt

Directions:

Chop onion and green pepper. You might run them through the blender or food processor at home and take them to camp in a zip-locked bag or other sealable container. Brown ground beef, add all other ingredients and simmer for about 30 minutes.

Serve on toasted hamburger buns or tortillas.

Seminole Hamburger

This one impresses the kids in camp. Anything Indian usually does.

Ingredients:
1 lb ground beef
salt and pepper to taste
1 1/2 cup self rising flour
oil for frying
1/2 cup chopped onion
1 cup pumpkin, cooked, mashed
water to make a soft dough

Directions:
Mix the ground beef, onions, salt and pepper together and set aside.

Mix pumpkin, flour and just enough water to make a soft dough. Knead the dough for a few minutes. Separate into 3-inch balls. Continue kneading, turning and pulling until the dough is elastic and about 1/4 inch thick and flat. Fill each piece of dough with a hamburger patty and seal well on all sides. Fry in deep fat or oil until golden brown on all sides. Serve immediately.

"Spicy" Ham Rolls

Nothing like a little finger food in camp.

Ingredients:
8 oz cream cheese
1 lb Danish ham, sliced
1 small bottle horseradish

Directions:
Mix horseradish and cream cheese until smooth. Spread on ham slices. Cut ham into quarters and roll each piece separately. Stick toothpicks into each ham roll and serve.

Deviled Ham Whip

Made up ahead of time and kept on ice, this mixture can produce some tasty sandwiches in a hurry.

Ingredients:
8 oz cream cheese, softened
3 oz can deviled ham
1 tbs pimento, chopped
½ cup relish spread
¼ cup diced green peppers
1 tbs grated onion

Directions:
Combine all ingredients and beat until well blended. Use as a sandwich spread.

Southwestern Sandwiches

This can be either breakfast or lunch, depending on your mood.

Ingredients:
¼ lb boiled ham, chopped
2 tbs chopped onions
⅛ tsp pepper
3 eggs, beaten
4 tortillas, heated
2 tbs chopped green pepper
dash of salt
¼ tsp celery seed
2 tbs butter or margarine

Directions:
In medium bowl, toss ham with green pepper, onion, salt, pepper and celery seed. Add eggs, mix well.

Heat butter in large skillet. Use 1/3 cup ham mixture for each sandwich. Cook until nicely browned on underside; turn; cook until other side is browned. Serve on tortillas.

Kaseschnitten

Ingredients:
4 slices bread
2 slices ham
dill pickle slices
dash paprika
butter
6 slice swiss cheese
1 oz white wine
2 fried eggs

Directions:

   Toast a slice of heavy bread in butter in a pan on both sides. Put a slice of ham on the bread. Add a slice of thin swiss cheese (several very thin slices work well).You can put some pickle slices between the ham and cheese also. Top with slice of bread. Set aside while frying eggs the way you like them. Set eggs aside.

   Put sandwiches in pan on a moderate heat and cover a minute or so. Be careful not to burn the cheese, which will begin to melt. Then raise the lid and add about a half oz of dry white wine quickly and snap the cover back on for a few moments (20-30 seconds). This steams the whole affair. Slide it onto a plate. Add some paprika on top and the fried egg.

Ginger-Pork Burgers

Ingredients:
1 lb ground pork
1 egg
1 tsp powdered garlic
½ cup oatmeal
small onion, chopped
1 tbs powdered ginger
up to 1 cup warm water

Directions:

Mix all ingredients together, except for the water. Add just enough water to make the mixture workable without being too gooey. Shape into burger patties, and pan fry. This is a nice change of pace.

Spicy Barbecue Wings

Ingredients:

½ lbs chicken wings
BBQ sauce
½ cup ketchup
½ cup water
2 tbs Dijon musard
1 tsp salt
2 tsp Louisiana hot sauce
½ tsp chili powder
2 garlic cloves - minced
¼ cup lemon Juice
1 tbs brown sugar
2 tbs oil
2 tbs worcestershire sauce
¼ tsp cumin
1 tsp black pepper
oil - for deep frying

Directions:

This BBQ sauce is mild. If you like hotter wings, add more Louisiana hot sauce.

In a saucepan, mix together BBQ sauce ingredients. Bring to a boil, then reduce heat and simmer for 15 minutes.

In a frying pan or wok, heat oil until hot. Deep fry a few wings at a time, until they are cooked through, about 10-15 minutes. Drain fried wings on absorbent towel. When all the wings are cooked, place them in the simmering BBQ sauce. Stir to coat and serve.

Buttermilk Batter Onion Rings

Ingredients:
1 egg
¼ tsp Tabasco Sauce
½ tsp salt
peanut oil for deep frying
coarse salt
1 cup buttermilk
1 cup all purpose flour
½ tsp baking soda

Directions:
   Peel and slice the onions into very thin slices. Separate into rings. Make the buttermilk batter. For the batter, beat together the egg, buttermilk and Tabasco (If Used). Sift together the dry ingredients and stir in until the batter is light. Let stand for at least 1 hour. Stir again before using.

   Heat the oil to 375 degrees F. Dip the onion slices in the batter, and fry in the oil, a few at a time. Remove from the oil when golden brown (About 5 Minutes). The oil temperature will drop when the onions are added then rise as the onions cook; regulate the heat accordingly. Drain on paper towels, sprinkle with coarse salt and serve at once.

Dinner

Chilies Rellenos (Stuffed Peppers)

Ingredients:
4 bell peppers
2 green onions, minced
1 tsp minced garlic
½ tsp thyme
½ tsp minced cilantro
¼ cup grated Monterey Jack
½ cup flour
oil for frying
1 tbs lard
2 tbs finely minced onions
4 oz ground chuck
1 tbs minced parsley
1 tbs raisins
6 oz flat beer
1 egg, beaten = 1 beaten white
salt and pepper to taste

Directions:
Blacken the peppers over an open flame. When cracked and black, put into a paper or plastic bag (wait a minute if using plastic). Secure the bag and let stand for 30 minutes. Peel the peppers. Make a slit lengthwise down the pepper and carefully remove the seeds. Melt the lard in a pan and add the minced onions, green onions, garlic and ground beef. Cook over high heat until well browned. Pour off excess fat and toss in the thyme, parsley, cilantro and raisins. Heat through and divide the mixture among half of the peppers. Secure with toothpicks and stuff the remaining peppers with grated cheese. Beat the beer into the flour and add the egg to form a batter. Let stand for at least 30 minutes, correcting the texture with an additional egg yolk or more flour. Heat the oil to 350 degrees. Dip each pepper into the batter allowing excess to run off. Fry the peppers until golden, drain well and serve one of each pepper per person.

Mexican Beef Dinner

Ingredients:
SAUCE
½ cup onion, chopped fine
3 tbs olive oil
½ cup water
2 tbs chili powder
½ tsp oregano
1 garlic clove - crushed
1 can tomato sauce (10 oz)
1 tbs flour
1 tsp salt
½ tsp cumin
MEAT
1 lb boneless chuck, cubed
10 oz baby lima beans
1 green pepper, in rings
1 can kernel corn, drained
1 onion, rings, separated
CONDIMENTS
1 cup cheddar cheese, shredded
¼ cup green onion, chopped

Directions:
Prepare the sauce by browning the onions and garlic on the oil. Add the remaining ingredients and simmer for 10 minutes, stirring occasionally. Tear off four 12 inch lengths of extra wide aluminum foil. On each length of foil place ¼ of the meat, top with ¼ of the vegetables and pour over ¼ of the sauce. Bring the edges of the foil up and leaving room for the expansion of the steam, seal well with a double fold wrap. Turn ends tightly. Place the packets in hot coals of campfire and cook until the meat is tender (1 to 1½ hours), turning the packets frequently. When the packets are ready to serve, cut open and top each with ¼ of the cheese and green onion.

Carne Gisada Con Papas (Meat & Potatoes)

Ingredients:
1 lb round steak, ½" thick
4 oz tomato sauce
1 tps salt
½ tsp ground pepper
1 large clove garlic, smashed
1 lb potatoes
½ tsp ground cumin
1 water

Directions:
Cut round steak into cubes and brown in shortening in heavy skillet. Peel and cube potatoes (approximately in ½ inch cubes). Once meat is slightly browned, add potatoes and continue to brown. (Don't worry if it sticks to the bottom of the skillet.) Add tomato sauce, salt, pepper, cumin powder and garlic. Add approximately one cup of water and simmer until meat and potatoes are tender. Potatoes will thicken sauce.

Beef And Tequila Stew

Ingredients:
1 lb meat*
⅛ cup vegetable oil
2 bacon slices, cut up
⅛ cup celery; chopped
½ cup tomato juice
½ tsp salt
2 cups tomatoes; chopped
⅛ cup unbleached flour
¼ cup onion; chopped
⅛ cup carrot; chopped
⅛ cup tequila
1 tsp cilantro snipped
15 oz garbanzo beans can
2 cloves garlic, minced

*Meat should be beef boneless chuck, tip or round, cut into 1-inch cubes. Coat beef with flour. Heat oil in 10-inch skillet until hot. Cook and stir beef in oil over medium heat until brown. Remove beef cubes and drain. Cook and stir onion and bacon in same skillet until bacon is crisp. Stir in beef and remaining ingredients. Heat to boiling; reduce heat. Cover and simmer until beef is tender, about 1 hour.

Beef Curry

Ingredients:
1½ lb beef chuck, cubed
flour
2 large onions, minced
¾ tsp ground coriander
½ tsp ground cumin seed
½ cup tomato juice
chutney
salt and pepper
2 tbs butter or margarine
1 cup boiling water
½ tsp tea, turmeric
cayenne pepper to taste
hot cooked rice

Directions:
Combine salt and pepper with the flour and roll the beef cubes, coating well. Brown the floured meat in the butter in a hot kettle. Remove meat and add the diced onions to the kettle, cooking until onions are soft and transparent. Add meat and the 1 cup boiling water, and spices to the kettle.

Bring to a boil and simmer for about 2 hours or until meat is tender. Stir in tomato juice. Serve over rice.

Crunchy Bean Sprouts with Beef

Ingredients:
½ lb flank steak
½ medium yellow onion
½ cup chicken stock
1 tbs dry sherry
2 tsp salt
2 cup bean sprouts
1 tbs peanut oil
1 tbs dark soy sauce
cornstarch paste
1 tsp Szechuan peppercorns

Directions:
Preparation: Rinse bean sprouts; drain. Separate layers of onion and slice into thin strips to match sprouts. Cut steak into slices across the grain ¼″ wide by 2″ long. Mix stock, soy sauce and sherry in a cup.

Prepare Szechuan pepper/salt: Heat dry wok to medium and add Szechuan peppercorns, stirring constantly until peppercorns exude a strong aroma; remove from heat. Crush peppercorns with salt, using rolling pin. Sift to remove coarse pieces. Store in closed jar.

Scalding: In large bowl, cover onions with boiling water; drain in 10 minutes. Add sprouts, cover both with boiling water; drain in 3 minutes. Sprinkle with about ½ tsp. Szechuan pepper/salt.

Stir-fry: Add oil to hot skillet. When oil starts to smoke, add steak, and stir-fry briskly for 1 minute or until meat loses pinkness. Push meat aside; add stock mixture and bring to boil. Dribble in thin cornstarch paste until light gravy is formed. Mix with beef. Pour over sprouts and onions in a serving bowl. Serve.

Beef and Broccoli with Garlic Sauce

Ingredients:
1 lb beef steak
½ tsp salt
1½ lb broccoli
1 tsp sesame oil
2 tbs vegetable oil
1 tbs finely chopped garlic
2 tbs brown bean sauce
1 tbs vegetable oil
dash of white pepper
1 tsp cornstarch
¼ cup chicken broth
1 tbs vegetable oil
1 tsp chopped gingerroot
1 cup sliced bamboo shoots

Directions

Trim fat from beef steak; cut beef lengthwise into 2-inch strips. Cut strips crosswise into ⅛-inch slices. Toss beef, 1 tbs vegetable oil, the salt and white pepper in a glass or plastic bowl. Cover and refrigerate 30 minutes. Pare outer layer from broccoli stems. Cut broccoli lengthwise into 1-inch stems; remove flowerets. Cut stems into 1-inch pieces. Place broccoli in boiling water; heat to boiling. Cover and cook 2 minutes; drain. Immediately rinse in cold water; drain. Mix cornstarch, sesame oil and broth. Heat 12-inch skillet or wok until very hot. Add 2 tbs vegetable oil; rotate skillet to coat bottom. Add beef; stir-fry 2 minutes or until beef is brown. Remove beef from skillet.

Heat skillet until very hot. Add 1 tbs vegetable oil; rotate skillet to coat bottom. Add garlic, gingerroot and bean sauce; stir-fry 30 seconds. Add bamboo shoots; stir-fry 1 minute. Stir in beef and broccoli. Stir in cornstarch mixture; cook and stir 15 seconds or until thickened.

Beef Tips on Rice

Ingredients:

3 tbs flour
1/2 tsp pepper
2 lb sirloin, cubed
2 tbs oil
3/4 cup water, boiling
1 tsp salt
1/2 tsp paprika
2 lg. onions, chopped
1 cube beef bouillon
Cooked rice

Directions:

Combine first 4 ingredients together in a small bowl. Dredge steak in flour. Saute' onions in oil. Add beef and cook until brown. Dissolve bouillon cube in water and add to beef. Cover and simmer 1½ hours stirring twice. Serve over cooked rice or noodles.

Easy Skillet Supper

Ingredients:

½ lb ground beef
½ cup chopped onions
cooking oil
salt and pepper
2 cup hash brown potatoes
4 eggs
1 cup grated longhorn cheese

Directions:

Crumble beef into skillet; brown in cooking oil. Add onions and potatoes, mixing well. Season to taste. Cook until onions are transparent and potatoes are brown. Stir frequently. Beat eggs and mix with grated cheese. Smooth meat and potato mixture in pan, pressing down gently. Pour egg and cheese mixture over top and cover. Cook until eggs are firm.

Western Skillet Rice

Ingredients:
1 lb ground beef
1½ cup water
16 oz can tomatoes
1 cup sharp cheese, shredded
1 env. dry onion soup mix
¾ cup uncooked rice
1 cup green peas

Directions:

Brown meat and drain. Add soup mix, water, rice, tomatoes and peas. Simmer 25 minutes until rice is tender. Top with shredded cheese before serving.

Southwest Beef & Rice

Ingredients:
1 12 oz can beef and gravy
4 oz Spanish rice
4 tsp tomato paste
3 cups water
1 cup instant rice
salt and pepper

Directions:

In a large pan, bring water to boil. Add tomato paste and blend. Add Spanish rice and cook for 6 or 7 minutes. Add beef and stir; cooking for about 3 minutes. Add instant rice. Remove from flame and allow to thicken for 5 minutes. Serve.

One-Pot Ground Beef Meals

Here are eight recipes in one. They all use the same basic ground beef base.

1½ lbs ground beef
½ green pepper, chopped
salt and pepper to taste
1 medium chopped onion
1 can condensed tomato soup

Directions:

Brown ground beef. Add the other ingredients except those required for combinations below. Simmer until thoroughly heated.

Add to this base any of the following to make:

- Yum Yums: Mix in 1/2 teaspoon chili powder, serve on or in buns
- Campers' Spaghetti: 1 16-oz can of spaghetti
- Spanish Rice: Small package of instant rice added while base is browning
- Macaroni and Cheese: ½ pound of macaroni and cheese cooked separately
- Hunters' Stew: 2 10½-oz cans condensed vegetable soup (undiluted)
- Chili: 1 16-oz can red beans and chili powder to taste
- Squaw Corn: 1 16-oz can whole-kernel corn and ½ pound of diced or shredded cheese
- Hungarian Hot Pot: 1 16-oz can baked beans

Meal in a Fry Pan

Ingredients:

1 lb ground beef
1 lb can tomatoes
1 tsp salt
1 tsp mustard
2 tbs onion, chopped
2 (1 lb) cans pork and beans
¼ tsp pepper

Directions:

Brown ground beef, drain excess fat. Add remaining ingredients and heat through. Serve immediately.

Cajun Style Chili

Ingredients:

1 lb of hamburger meat
3 tbs of red pepper
3 tbs of parsley
½ of an onion
4 whole peppers
4 oz can of tomato sauce
1½ tsp of salt
3 tbs of pepper
1½ tsp of Italian seasoning
4 green onions
1 can ranch style beans
1½ tbs chili powder

Directions:

Brown hamburger; drain any fat. Add onions and all seasons. When onions are soft add the ranch style beans. Save the Chili powder for when you put the beans in. Add about 5 to 6 cups of water with the beans. Then add the tomato sauce. This is going to be very hot. If you can not handle it hot cut back on the peppers and pepper powder. Let this cook about 1½ hours on low. You will have to add more water as it cooks.

Earl's Hurry-up Chili

Ingredients:
1 lb ground beef
3 tbs dried minced onions
1½ tsp oregano powder
1 (16 oz) can kidney beans
1 soup can of water
1 tbs garlic powder
1 pkg Texas red chili seasoning
14 oz can crushed tomato puree
1 (10 oz) can tomato soup
salt to taste

Directions:
   In a large pot, brown the ground beef along with the garlic powder, minced onions, chili seasoning, and oregano. Open the cans while it is browning.
   When the meat and seasonings are nicely browned, add the crushed tomatoes, the kidney beans (juice and all), and the whole can of tomato soup. Stir well. Next, grab that soup can and fill it with hot water. Pour in water until the chili is just about the consistency you like. Stir it all again, and get a small spoonful to check the taste for salt. Reduce heat and simmer for about 20 minutes, stirring often enough to keep it from sticking on the bottom of the pot.

Mom's Chili

Ingredients:
1 lb ground chuck
1 tsp garlic powder
2 cups water
½ tsp paprika
1½ tsp onion powder
8 oz can of tomato sauce
1 tbs chili powder
1 can red kidney beans

Directions:

Brown the hamburger in pot and drain. Add salt, pepper, onion powder and garlic powder to taste. Add the tomato sauce, water, chili powder and paprika. Stir well. Put on stove after lunch and let simmer covered for 4 hours. Remove lid and add entire can of beans. Place on stove at low-medium heat until mixture heats thoroughly.

Hearty Hodgepodge

Ingredients:

1 lb ground beef
1 8 oz can lima beans
1 8 oz can peas, drained
1 4 oz can mushrooms
1 tbs sugar
1½ tsp salt
¼ cup milk
½ tsp garlic salt
1 onion, chopped
1 green pepper, chopped
1 16-oz can tomatoes
3 oz pkg cream cheese
½ tsp pepper

Directions:

Brown ground beef in skillet. Drain well. Add all remaining ingredients except cream cheese and milk. Stir well. Combine cream cheese and milk and mix thoroughly. Spread cream cheese mixture over top. Cover and keep cool overnight. In the morning, cover and simmer all day or put on high after lunch and cook for at least 4 hours.

Goulash, Hungarian Style

This is also nice cooked with potatoes and served with boiled, buttered noodles

Ingredients:
3 tbs margarine
2 potatoes, peeled, quartered
salt and pepper
1 cup water
3 cup sliced onions
1 lb beef, cubed
2 tsp paprika

Directions:
In a large skillet, over medium high heat, melt the butter and cook the onion until golden (5-6 minutes). With a slotted spoon remove the onion and put it in the pot. Place the potatoes on the onion. Add meat to the skillet and saute until well browned on all sides. Sprinkle the meat with salt and pepper and lift into the pot. Add the water to the skillet, scrape up the pan juices, and pour it all into the pot. Cover and simmer all day, or until tender.

Stove Top Meat Loaf

Ingredients:
½ cup whole or condensed milk
1 lb ground beef
1 small onion, peeled
½ tsp pepper
1 can (12 oz) whole tomatoes
2 slices white bread
2 eggs
1½ tsp salt
1 tsp dry mustard

Directions:
Place the milk and bread in a large mixing bowl, and let stand until the bread has absorbed all the

milk. With two forks, break the bread into crumbs. Mix the ground beef into the crumbs. Make a hollow in the center of the meat and break the eggs into it. Beat the eggs a little, then grate the onion into the eggs. Add salt, pepper and mustard.

Beat the eggs into the beef. Shape into a round cake and place in the pot. Drain the tomatoes and place them on the meat. Cover and simmer for 5-7 hours.

Before serving: Uncover pot; turn the heat to high and boil away some of the sauce. It should be thick, not thin.

Earl's Goulash

Whip this up while your making lunch and let it simmer while you're out fishing or hunting during the afternoon

Ingredients:
1 lb ground beef
16 oz can whole tomatoes, undrained and chopped
3 cups water
3 oz frozen cut okra
1 ½ cups chopped onion
½ tsp Worcestershire sauce
½ tsp salt
¼ tsp black pepper
hot cooked rice (if desired)

Directions:
Cook ground beef in a big pot until meat is browned. Drain well. Add tomatoes and remaining ingredients (except rice) and stir well. Bring to boil; reduce heat, and simmer uncovered for about 3 hours. Depending on your field stove, the ingredients may thicken in under 3 hours, or it may take a little longer. If you have cooked up some rice, serve over it.

Hamburger Casserole

Ingredients:
2 large potatoes, sliced
2 medium carrots, sliced
1 stalk celery, sliced
2 medium onions, sliced
1 lb lean ground beef, browned
1 can peas, drained
1 can tomato soup
1 soup can water

Directions:
Place layers of vegetables in the order given in pot. Season each layer with salt and pepper. Put the lightly browned ground beef on top of the celery. Mix the tomato soup with the water and pour into pot. Cover and simmer all day, stirring occasionally.

Meat Spaghetti Sauce

Ingredients:
½ lb pork sausage
1 cup chopped onion
½ lb fresh mushrooms, sliced
8 oz can tomato sauce
1 tsp salt
1 tsp oregano leaves
½ tsp marjoram leaves
1 cup water
½ lb ground chuck
½ cup chopped parsley
6 oz can tomato paste
½ cup dry red wine
1 tsp rosemary
½ tsp black pepper
½ tsp garlic powder

Directions:

Brown meats in skillet, drain off fat. Combine meat and remaining ingredients in pot and mix well. Cover and simmer all day.

Brisket Dinner

Ingredients:

1 lb brisket of beef
½ tsp whole thyme
1 cup small boiling onions
½ tsp salt
1 bay leaf
1 cup water
1 large onion, chopped
1 large carrot, chopped
3 medium carrots, in strips

Directions:

Place brisket in pot. Add chopped onion, chopped carrot, salt, bay leaf, thyme and water. Cover and simmer all day. When meat is done, lift gently from stock. Support underneath with spatula; keep warm. Add small onions and carrots to stock in pot. Cover and cook on high for 1 to 2 hours. Remove vegetables from broth with a slotted spoon and arrange around meat.

Brisket of Beef with Beans

Ingredients:

1 lb beef brisket
¾ tsp salt
2 cup water
⅛ cup maple syrup or molasses
½ tsp dry mustard
2 slices bacon
½ tsp ground black pepper
½ lb navy beans soaked
¼ cup packed brown sugar

Directions:

Drain the beans. Brown the fat side of the brisket in a skillet over medium-high heat. Add the bacon or oil, and brown the other side. Add the salt, pepper, water and beans. Reduce heat to medium, and cook, covered for 2 hours or until the beef and beans are tender. stirring occasionally to prevent sticking. Remove the beef and keep warm. Add the maple syrup or molasses, brown sugar and mustard to the beans. Mix thoroughly, and simmer over medium heat for another 10 minutes. Slice the brisket thin and serve with the beans.

Old Settler's Stew

Ingredients:

1 lb boneless beef brisket
1 lb potatoes
½ lb onions, diced large
¼ lb celery, diced large
1 cup canned tomatoes
3 carrots
¼ lb green peas
salt and pepper

Directions:

Cut the beef in two-inch chunks and put them in a

skillet or other pan, just covered with water. Cook over the fire until the beef is tender, about 2½ hours. Add potatoes and carrots and cook another 30 minutes.

Now add the onions, peas and celery and cook for about 15 minutes. Add tomatoes and salt and pepper to taste and cook for another 15 minutes before serving.

Mountain Man Beef Skillet

Ingredients:
1 lb lean ground beef
1½ tsp chili powder
½ teaspoon garlic salt
15½ oz (1 can) kidney beans
¾ cup water
¾ cup onion, chopped
cheddar cheese, shredded
½ teaspoon salt
16 oz whole tomatoes, cut up
¾ cup rice (uncooked)
3 tbs green pepper, chopped
corn chips

Directions:

Cook ground beef and onion in large skillet until beef is browned and onion is tender. Drain fat and discard. Add chili powder, salt and garlic salt to meat mixture. Stir in undrained tomatoes and beans, raw rice, water and green pepper. Cover and simmer, stirring occasionally, for 20 minutes. Top with cheese and chips if desired.

Beef Easy Supper Dish

Ingredients:
2 tbs butter or margarine
1 onion, chopped fine
1 tsp sugar
½ lb ground beef
2 cups tomato juice
1 tsp salt
1 cup uncooked elbow macaroni
1 cup cubed cheddar cheese

Directions:
Melt butter in sauce pan over low heat. Add macaroni and stir to coat thoroughly. Add two cups of tomato juice and bring to rapid boil. Stir in ground beef. Add salt, pepper, and sugar. Cover, reduce heat and cook for 20 minutes. Remove cover and stir. Sprinkle cheese on top. Remove from heat and cover so cheese will melt. All you need is a salad for a meal for two.

Macaroni Skillet Supper

Ingredients:
2 tbs butter
¾ cup chopped onion
¼ cup chopped green pepper
1 teaspoon salt
1 cup uncooked elbow macaroni
¾ cup shredded cheddar cheese
1 pound lean ground beef
½ cup chopped celery
1 lb 12 oz can tomatoes
¼ teaspoon pepper
½ cup grated parmesan cheese
Chopped parsley

Directions:
In a large skillet with cover melt butter; add beef,

onion, celery and green pepper and saute until meat is browned. Add tomatoes, salt and pepper; bring to boil. Add macaroni; cover and cook over low heat, stirring occasionally, for 10 minutes or until macaroni is tender. Stir in parmesan cheese. Sprinkle with cheddar cheese; cover and allow to stand for 5 minutes. Sprinkle with parsley and serve.

Chicken Curry

Ingredients:
4 pieces chicken
1 pepper, freshly ground
3 tbs oil
1½ tbs curry powder
2 cups chicken stock
½ cup golden raisins
salt to taste
½ tsp cinnamon, ground
2 onions, small, fine chopped
1½ tbs all-purpose flour
2 tart green apples

Directions:
Peel and chop up the apples. Wash chicken pieces and pat dry with paper towels. Sprinkle with salt, pepper and cinnamon. Heat oil in large, heavy frying pan and brown chicken quickly on all sides. Remove chicken from pan. Add the onions to pan and saute until transparent. Sprinkle with curry powder and flour and cook, stirring for 2 minutes. Stir in chicken stock and bring to a boil. Add chicken, cover and simmer very gently for 30 - 40 minutes, or until tender. About 5 minutes before chicken is done, add apples and raisins and continue cooking. Serve chicken with sauce. Serve with rice.

Golden Mushroom Chicken Thighs

Ingredients:
6 chicken thighs
1 can golden mushroom soup

Directions:
   Put chicken in pot. Pour in one can of golden mushroom soup and 1 can water. Cover pot and cook on high heat for about 4 hours or until chicken falls off bone. Remove bones and serve with rice or noodles.

Chicken and Rice Dinner

Ingredients:
1 lb chicken pieces, skinned
2 carrots; peeled, sliced ½″
½ cup onion, chopped
1 tsp bouillon, chicken, granules
1 sm. can mushrooms, sliced
½ cup rice, long grain
1 tsp poultry seasoning
¼ tsp salt

Directions:
   Spray a 12-inch skillet with nonstick spray coating. Brown chicken pieces on all sides over medium heat about 15 minutes. Remove chicken. Drain fat from skillet, if necessary. Add mushrooms, carrots, rice, onion, bouillon, poultry seasoning, 2 cups water, salt. Place chicken atop rice mixture. Cover; simmer 30 minutes or till chicken and rice are done.

Stir-Fried Chicken and Chinese Cabbage

Ingredients:
¼ lb boneless chicken breast*
2 green onions in 1-inch lengths
2 cloves garlic, crushed
2 tbs soy sauce
1 tsp sugar
1 tbs sesame or salad oil
3 cup Chinese cabbage, sliced
1 tbs fresh ginger, chopped
1/3 cup water, chicken broth
2 tsp cornstarch
2 tsp rice or cider vinegar

*Boneless pork cutlet can be substituted for chicken

Directions:

Slice the meat across the grain into thin strips and place on a plate near the cooking area. Prepare the Chinese cabbage, onion, ginger, and garlic as indicated and arrange on plate with chicken.

In a measuring cup or small bowl, combine the water, soy sauce, cornstarch, sugar, and vinegar; stir to dissolve the cornstarch and sugar. Place by meat and vegetables.

Preheat a heavy 10-inch saute pan, non-reactive skillet, or wok on high heat for about 1 minute. Add oil and tilt pan to coat evenly; add chicken. Cook, turning constantly, for 1 minute. Add cabbage, green onion, ginger, and garlic; continue cooking and stirring another minute. Stir in the liquid mixture; cook and stir until the sauce is thickened and the vegetables are tender-crisp and brightly colored, about 30 seconds more.

Serve over hot cooked rice.

Chicken Creole

Ingredients:
¾ cup onion - chopped
1 cup tomato - chopped
1 bay leaf
1 tbs parsley - fresh, minced
pinch cayenne
½ cup green pepper, chopped
2 clove garlic, minced
½ tsp thyme
⅛ tsp black pepper
6 oz chicken breasts

Directions:
  In a saucepan, over high heat, cook the onion and bell pepper, stirring regularly until they begin to color. Add all remaining ingredients, including the chicken breasts. Cover and simmer gently for 10 minutes.

Chicken Skillet Dinner

Ingredients:
1 cup chicken, cooked, pieces
16 oz can peas
2 tbs cooking oil
1 green pepper, cut in strips
1 tomato, cut in wedges
½ cup tomato puree
½ cup potatoes, cooked, diced
16 oz can whole kernel corn
1 onion, sliced
1 tbs worcestershire sauce
1 can cream mushroom soup

Directions:
  Saute onions and green pepper in skillet until soft. Add chicken, potatoes, corn, peas and tomato; heat through. Combine soup, tomato puree, and 1 cup of

water. Add to mixture in skillet. Salt and pepper to taste. Bring to boil and cook for six minutes while stirring.

Chicken Poached with Vegetables and Herbs

Ingredients:
4 pieces chicken
1 tsp salt
3 strips bacon, minced
4 carrot, peeled, grated
2 peppercorns, crushed
¼ tsp dried thyme
1 tbs all purpose flour
⅛ tsp pepper
1 onion, peeled, chopped
1 tart apple, peeled, cubed
½ bay leaf
½ cup dry rosé wine

Directions:
Sprinkle the chicken pieces with flour combined with salt and pepper. In a large skillet, over medium heat, stir the bacon bits until crisp. Turn the onion, carrot and apple into the bacon and saute until the onion is transparent. Add the peppercorns, bay leaf, thyme, and pat the mixture into the bottom of a pot. Press the chicken pieces on top and pour the wine over all. You can substitute orange juice or water for the wine. Cover and simmer 5-7 hours.

Baja Chicken Pasta Salad

Ingredients:

¾ lb chicken breast
1 cup ring macaroni
½ cup mayonnaise
1 tsp red chilies; ground
6 oz dried mixed fruit
2 green onions/tops; sliced
2 tbs plain yogurt
¼ tsp salt

Directions:

Heat enough salted water to cover the chicken breast (¼ tsp salt to 1 cup of water) to boiling in a pot. Add the chicken breast. Cover and heat to boiling, reduce the heat and simmer until the chicken is done, about 15 to 20 minutes. Remove the chicken with a slotted spoon. Heat the water to boiling and add the fruit and ring macaroni or orzo gradually so that the water continues to boil. Boil uncovered, stirring occasionally, just until the ring macaroni is tender, about 6 to 8 minutes or 10 minutes for the orzo, then drain. Rinse with cold water and drain again. Cut the chicken into 1/2-inch pieces and mix with the fruit, macaroni, and onions. Mix the remaining ingredients and toss with the chicken mixture. Let cool before serving.

Pot-Roasted Pork

Ingredients:
1 lb loin end pork roast
salt and pepper
1 clove garlic, sliced
2 medium onions, sliced
½ bay leaves
1 whole clove
1 cup hot water
2 tbs soy sauce

Directions:
   Rub pork roast with salt and pepper. Make tiny slits in meat and insert slivers of garlic. Brown roast on all sides in pot. Remove roast. Put 1 sliced onion in bottom of pot. Add browned pork roast and remaining onion and other ingredients. Cover and simmer all day.
   To thicken gravy: Remove roast to serving platter. Blend 2 tablespoons cornstarch with 2 tablespoons cold water to form smooth paste. Turn up heat and pour in paste. Stir well and let come to boil-about 15 minutes-until thickened.

Quick Skillet Sausage

Ingredients:
1 lb bulk pork sausage
3 cups cooked rice
1 to 3 tbs chopped Jalapeno pepper
1 medium onion, chopped
1 15 oz can pinto beans

Directions:
   In a 10″ skillet,cook sausage until brown,stirring to crumble. Pour off fat and return 2 tbs to skillet.Add onion and cook until soft but not brown. Stir in rice, beans and Jalapeno pepper; heat thoroughly.

Stir-fried Pork and Asparagus

This is a basic stir-fried vegetable and meat dish.

Ingredients:

¼ lb boneless pork butt
½ tsp fresh ginger root, minced
1/3 cup chicken stock
2 tsp oyster sauce
12 medium asparagus spears
1 tbs peanut oil
1 pinch sugar
thin cornstarch paste

Directions:

Preparation: Slice pork butt (or comparable boneless pork) across the grain into strips 2″ by ¼″ by ⅛″ thick. Wash and trim tough white skin from asparagus. Cut asparagus into 2½″ segments. If asparagus is thick (¾″ or more), cut on bias so it will cook quickly and be balanced in size with pork strips.

Stir-frying: Heat peanut oil in frying pan until it just begins to smoke. Add pork strips and stir-fry about 1 minute until no longer pink. Add asparagus and stir-fry briskly for another minute. Before asparagus turns bright green, add ginger, chicken stock and sugar; keep stirring. When liquid boils, reduce heat to medium, add oyster sauce, cover and simmer for about 1 minute or until asparagus is cooked but still firm. Uncover, turn up heat, and push ingredients out of liquid. Dribble in cornstarch paste, stirring continuously until liquid thickens. You may need 1 to 2 tsp of paste. Recombine ingredients. Serve.

Curried Pork with Sweet Potatoes

Ingredients:
2 large sweet potatoes
1 onion
2 tbs sesame oil
½ tablespoon salt
1 cup stock
oil for stir fry (peanut)
1 lb pork
1 or 2 slices fresh ginger root
1 tbs soy sauce
dash of pepper
2 tbs curry powder

Directions:

Peel sweet potatoes and cut in ½ inch slices. Cut pork in ½ inch cubes. Slice onion thin. Mince ginger root. Heat oil and deep-fry sweet potatoes until light golden. Drain on paper toweling. Heat remaining oil. Add ginger root and onion and stir-fry a few times. Add pork and brown lightly on all sides. Stir in soy sauce, salt and pepper. Then add stock and curry powder and bring to a boil stirring. Add deep fried potatoes and simmer, covered, until pork is done (30-40 minutes.)

Twice Cooked Pork and Spicy Vegetables

Twiced-cooked pork in its many versions is a typical dish of southwestern China.

Ingredients:
½ lb pork butt in one piece
2 large cloves garlic, minced
1 small bell pepper
1 large carrot
1/3 cup water
1 pinch sugar
2 tbs peanut oil
2 dried red chili, minced
2 tsp fresh ginger root, minced
¼ cup bamboo shoots
1 cube bean curd
1 tbs soy sauce
1 tsp salt
cornstarch paste

Directions:

In saucepan, cover pork butt with water, bring to a boil and simmer for 30 minutes. Add more hot water if level goes below pork. Cool pork in its cooking water. Halve, seed and core bell pepper; cut into pieces about 1″ by 1½″. Slice bamboo to match bell pepper. Peel carrot; slice on bias into ovals. Remove pork from cooking water, and parboil* carrots in water for 1 minute. Slice pork butt into rectangles same size as bell pepper. Combine water with soy sauce, sugar and salt. Drain bean curd, rinse in cold water, and slice same size as bell pepper. Bean curd can be left out for those who don't care for the taste.

Stir-fry: Add oil to very hot skillet. When oil begins to smoke, stir-fry garlic and ginger for 1 minute. Add bell pepper, bamboo shoots, carrots and pork; stir-fry for 1 minute. Add bean curd and mushroom liquid; bring to boil. On medium heat, cover and cook for 1-2

minutes, until bell pepper is bright green and crisp.
Push ingredients to side. Restir thick cornstarch
paste, then dribble into liquid until it thickens; cook
briefly while stirring. Recombine with ingredients.
Serve.

*Boil until partially cooked

Stir-Fried Cucumber with Pork

Ingredients:

1/4 lb pork butt, boned
1 clove garlic, minced
1/4 tsp salt
1 tbs sherry
1/2 cup chicken stock
1 large cucumber
2 tbs peanut oil
1 tbs thin soy sauce
1 pinch sugar
cornstarch paste

Directions:

Preparation: Slice pork butt across grain, then into
strips 1/4" thick by 2" long. Marinate with soy sauce,
sherry and sugar for 15 minutes. Peel cucumber; slice
in half the long way and remove seeds; slice in strips
to match pork; marinate in salt water for 15 minutes.

Stir-frying: Heat skillet or wok until very hot; add 1/2
of oil. Drain pork; save liquid. When oil just begins
to smoke, add pork and stir-fry rapidly for about 1
minute until shrivelled. Remove pork from skillet or
wok; wash skillet.

Reheat skillet until very hot; add remaining oil.
Drain cucumber. When oil just begins to smoke, add
cucumber and stir-fry rapidly until heated through
about 30 seconds. Add pork and garlic; stir briefly;
add stock. Bring stock to boil; then stir in enough
cornstarch paste to make a light gravy. Bring sauce
to boil. Serve.

Spicy Pork and Black Bean Chili

Ingredients:
½ lb black beans
½ lb boneless lean pork, cubed
5 garlic cloves, minced
½ tbs paprika
2 tsp cumin, ground
1 can tomatoes, chopped 14 oz
2 tbs red wine vinegar
1 tsp coriander
½ tsp black pepper
2 tbs olive oil
1 onion, large, chopped
1 tbs chili powder
1 tsp oregano, dried
½ tsp chili pepper flakes
1 cup chicken stock
1 green pepper, diced
½ tsp salt

Directions:

In a large pot, cover beans with water. Let stand over night. Drain liquid and cover with cold water. Bring to a boil, reduce heat and let simmer for about 1½ hours or until beans are tender. Drain and reserve.

Meanwhile, heat oil in a large saucepan on high heat and brown meat cubes on all sides. Remove from pan and set aside.

Add onions and garlic to pan; cook on medium heat until tender about 5 minutes. Add chili powder, paprika, oregano, cumin and chili pepper flakes; cook, stirring for 1 minute.

Return meat to pan along with tomatoes, including juice, stock and vinegar. Bring to boil, let simmer, partly covered, for 1½ hours or until meat is tender. Add beans and peppers; season with salt and pepper. Cover and cook 15 minutes more or until peppers are tender. Add coriander. Serve.

French Twist New England Boiled Dinner

Ingredients:

1 lb head of green cabbage
4 medium potatoes, peeled
2 leeks, trimmed & well washed
1 onion*
2 tsp allspice
1 bay leaf
1 salt to taste
1 lb smoked shoulder
4 carrots, trim & scrape
4 ribs celery, trimmed, tied
2 whole cloves *
1 tsp dried thyme
6 peppercorns
4 chicken legs and thighs

Directions:

*Peel onion but leave stem on, press cloves into onion.

Remove and discard any tough outer leaves on the cabbage, quarter and remove the core.

In large kettle, combine the pork butt, potatoes, cabbage, carrots, leeks, celery, onion, allspice, thyme, bay leaf, and peppercorns. Cover with water, add salt to taste. Cover, bring to a boil, reduce heat and simmer for 20 minutes. Add the chicken and simmer for 15 minutes more.

Spanish Pork Chop Dinner

Ingredients:
4 pork chops, trimmed of fat
1 tsp salt
¼ tsp black pepper
½ cup chopped onion
1 can whole tomatoes
½ cup grated Cheddar cheese
1 tbs oil
1 tsp chili powder
¾ cup long grain rice
¼ cup chopped green peppers
5 green pepper rings

Directions:
In large Dutch oven, slowly brown the chops in heated oil. Drain off excess oil. Sprinkle chops with salt, chili powder and black pepper. Add rice, onions and chopped green peppers. Pour in tomatoes with liquid, breaking tomatoes into pieces. Cover and bring to boiling over high heat. Reduce heat and simmer 35 to 40 minutes, stirring occasionally. Add pepper rings and cook 2 minutes longer or until rice and meat are tender. Sprinkle with cheese.

Creamy Ham and Beans

Ingredients:
1 can condensed cream of mushroom soup
½ lb boiled ham, cut into pieces
beans
½ cup shredded carrot
⅛ tsp black pepper
1 soup can milk
1 cup frozen cut green beans
½ tsp dry mustard
1 ½ cups dry rice

Directions:
Stir soup and milk in a skillet until smooth. Add

ham, carrot, beans, mustard and black pepper. Bring to a boil over medium heat. Reduce heat; cover and simmer 5 minutes or until beans are tender. Stir in rice. Cover; remove from heat. Let stand 5 minutes. Fluff with a fork. Makes 4 servings.

Kraut 'n' Pork Chops

Ingredients:
4 thick pork chops
salt and pepper to taste
shortening
1 can sauerkraut, drained
1 cup ketchup
1 tbs brown sugar

Directions:
   Sprinkle chops with salt and pepper. Heat shortening in a skillet. Brown chops lightly on both sides. Mix sauerkraut with ketchup. Arrange a mound of sauerkraut on top of each chop. Sprinkle with brown sugar. Cover and cook over low heat for 40 to 50 minutes.

Turkey Saute Marengo

Ingredients:
¼ cup dry white wine
2 tbs vegetable oil
1 lb turkey breast, in strips
2 cans stewed tomatoes
3/4 tsp garlic powder
½ tsp salt
2 tsp cornstarch
1 cup bell pepper, in strips
8 oz fresh mushrooms, halved
1 tsp thyme leaves, crushed
½ tsp grated orange peel
¼ tsp black pepper

Directions:
   In a custard cup combine wine and cornstarch until smooth; set aside. In a large skillet heat oil until hot. Add green pepper; cook and stir until almost crisp-tender, about two minutes. Stir in turkey and mushrooms; cook and stir until turkey is no longer pink, two to three minutes. Stir in tomatoes, thyme, garlic powder, orange peel, salt and black pepper; heat, stirring occasionally until hot, about two minutes. Add reserved wine mixture; cook and stir until mixture boils and thickens.

Quick Turkey Dinner

Ingredients:
1 lb ground raw turkey
1 cup cracker meal
½ cup Egg Beaters (= 2 eggs)
2 tbs margarine
16 oz can whole cranberry sauce
½ cup water
2 tsp instant chicken bouillon

Directions:

Combine turkey, cracker meal and Egg Beaters in small bowl until well blended. Shape into 8 oval patties. Melt margarine in large skillet over med-high heat. Brown patties on both sides. Blend cranberry sauce, water and bouillon; pour over patties. Bring to boil. Reduce heat, cover and simmer until done, about 20 minutes. Arrange patties on serving plate, spoon sauce over them. Serve with potatoes and vegetable of choice.

San Antonio-Style Turkey-Pasta Skillet

Ingredients:

10 oz vermicelli in pieces
2 garlic cloves, minced
16 oz can whole tomatoes
2 cups turkey, cooked, diced
1 tsp cumin ground
½ cup cheddar cheese, shredded
2 large onions coarsely chopped
¼ cup vegetable oil
14 oz can chicken broth
¾ cup picante sauce
1 large green pepper, in strips

Directions:

Cook onion and garlic in oil in skillet over medium heat for 2 minutes. Add pasta; cook and stir 2 minutes. Stir in tomatoes, broth and turkey.

Simmer, stirring occasionally and breaking up tomatoes with spoon, 3 minutes. Add green pepper; continue to simmer until pasta is tender and most of liquid is absorbed, 4 to 5 minutes. Sprinkle with cheese and if desired, cilantro. Serve with extra picante sauce.

Red Beans with Turkey Sausage

Ingredients:
1 lb dried red beans
2 quarts hot water
½ cup chopped green pepper
1 tsp cayenne pepper
1 bay leaf
1 lb smoked turkey sausage, in pieces
1 cup finely chopped onions
½ cup finely chopped celery
½ tsp salt

Directions:
In a large pot, place the beans and enough water to cover by 2 inches. Soak the beans overnight and drain thoroughly. To the same pot over medium heat, add all the remaining ingredients. Cover, and cook for 30 minutes, stirring often. Reduce the heat and simmer 30 minutes longer, or until the beans are tender. Remove the bay leaf and serve.

Fish & Game

FISH

Flounder Zucchini Saute

Flounder is a favorite fish among coastal campers.

Ingredients:
¾ lb flounder fillet
1 small zucchini sliced
1 clove garlic, minced
1 tomato, peeled, cut in wedges
1 tbs lemon juice
salt and pepper
¼ cup chopped onion
3 tbs oil, divided
1 tbs chopped parsley

Directions:
Sprinkle fish with salt and pepper. Saute zucchini, onion and garlic in 1 tbs oil for 2 minutes. Add tomato and parsley; cook covered 1 minute. Remove from pan. Saute fish in 2 tbs oil until brown on both sides. Allow a total cooking of 10 minutes per inch of thickness measured at thickest part or until fish flakes easily. Return vegetables to pan. Add lemon juice and salt and pepper to taste. Heat briefly.

Fresh Tuna Steaks

It is not likely that one would be involved in primitive camping in an area where the catch of the day would include tuna, but it is possible in the Florida Keys or Baja California.

If it happens, here is an Italian treatment of fresh tuna called Tonno alla Genovese in Italy. If you don't happen to catch a tuna, try steaks from any large fish like striped bass, cod, catfish or largemouth bass.

If you can't find Italian mushrooms, don't worry. Eliminate them or substitute domestic mushrooms. If anyone notices the difference, it would surprise me. Likewise, if the use of wine in cooking is against your religion or taste preference, substitute water or orange juice. There's no chance of intoxication from the wine because the alcohol is the first thing to go when it is used in cooking.

Ingredients:

1 oz dried Italian mushrooms
3 tbs olive oil
2 garlic cloves - chopped
1 cup white wine
salt and pepper to taste
juice of 1 lemon
¾ cup warm water
3 tsp parsley
1 tsp all-purpose flour
4 tuna steaks, ¾ inch thick
1 tbs butter

Directions:

Soak mushrooms in warm water for 20 minutes. Drain, saving liquid. Strain mushroom liquid. Rinse mushrooms under cold running water. Squeeze to remove as much moisture as possible. Heat oil in a large skillet. Add mushrooms, parsley, garlic, and flour. Stir over medium heat until garlic begins to color. Stir in wine. When wine is reduced by half, add tuna steaks. Season with salt and pepper. Cover and cook about 5 minutes. Gently turn tuna and cook 3 to 5 minutes or until fish can be flaked. Place fish on a warm platter. Keep warm. Add mushroom liquid you saved to skillet with butter and lemon juice. Cook over high heat until sauce has a medium-thick consistency. Spoon sauce over tuna. Serve immediately.

Canadian Indian Walleye Chowder

This is based on an old Sioux Indian recipe. I am sure the half and half is part of the adaptation.

Ingredients:
1 cup chopped onion
1 tbs salt
5 cup walleye, ¾" cubes
2 cup milk
4 cup cubed potatoes
⅛ tbs pepper
1 qt boiling water
1 cup half & half cream

Directions:
Add potatoes, onions, salt and pepper to water. Cook about 10 minutes, until vegetables are soft, but not completely cooked. Add fish and cook 10 minutes. Add milk and light cream, stir and heat 15 minutes longer. DO NOT BOIL.

Cajun Catfish

This is one of the ways catfish is prepared in Louisiana.

Ingredients:
4 catfish fillets
1 tbs paprika
¼ tsp onion powder
½ tsp cayenne pepper
½ tsp white pepper
1 tbs oil
1 oz wheat flakes cereal
¼ tsp salt
¼ tsp garlic powder
½ tsp black pepper
½ tsp thyme

Directions:

Wash the fish fillets and pat dry. In a bowl mix the ground wheat flakes and all the seasonings. Pour the dry mixture onto a piece of foil or wax paper, and dip the fillets into the seasoning, coating both sides.

In a skillet, heat the oil. Fry the fillets for 2 minutes on each side. Thick fillets may take a little longer to fry. Lay the fillets on a plate lined with a paper towel, cover with another paper towel, and pat to remove excess oil.

Speckled Trout Creole

In Louisiana, they use the abundant speckled sea trout in this recipe, but walleye, black bass, cod or striped bass are a few fish that will work just as well. Mix the spices ahead of time so that you are ready to cook just about any kind of fish.

Ingredients:
2 tbs salad oil
1 medium onion chopped
1 clove of garlic chopped
1 green pepper chopped
1 12 oz can tomatoes
1 tsp celery seed
1 bay leaf
1 tsp salt
2 tsp sugar
½ tsp chili powder
1 tbs chopped parsley
1 lb trout fillets, cut up

Directions:

In sauce pan, saute onion, garlic and pepper in margarine until soft. About 5 minutes. Add remaining ingredients and simmer uncovered for 45 minutes. Stir occasionally.

Sauted Salmon Steaks

Some of my West Coast friends give me a dirty look when I tell them I put salmon in a frying pan, but what else is a body to do in camp.

Ingredients:
4 salmon steaks
1 tsp soy sauce
1 tbs butter
¼ tsp garlic powder

Directions:
In a skillet, melt margarine and add soy sauce and garlic powder. Add salmon and cook 4-5 minutes. Turn and continue to cook 4-5 minutes or until fish flakes easily.

Fast and Fancy Bass Fillets

The recipe is for black bass, but other bass like striped bass, rock bass, sea bass will work just as well.

Ingredients:
1/3 cup butter
1 cup chablis
2 cup halved cherry tomatoes
3 shallots, minced
1 lb bass fillets
½ cup chopped watercress or parsley

Directions:
Melt butter in a large frying pan over medium heat. Stir in shallots; saute and stir for 2 minutes. Add chablis. When wine is warmed, add the fish fillets. Lower the heat and simmer, covered, for 7 minutes. Transfer the cooked fish to heated serving plates. Add the tomatoes to same pan; cook for 1 or 2 minutes until just heated through. Spoon tomato and wine sauce over fish fillets.

Grouper Fingers

While this is a popular way to serve grouper on the Bahamas Islands, it can be used to cook black bass, walleye, catfish or any of several saltwater fish, including flounder, sole and snapper.

Ingredients:
1 habanera pepper, minced
1 cup flour
½ cup milk (or more)
1 lb grouper fillets, in strips
2 eggs, beaten
cooking oil for frying

Directions:
Make a batter by mixing together the pepper, flour, eggs and milk. Dip the fingers in the batter and deep fry until golden brown.

Hungarian Shark Goulash

Catfish chunks are an excellent substitute for shark in this recipe.

Ingredients:
2 lb blacktip shark, bite-size chunks
1 green pepper
½ cup white wine
oil for sauteing
1 onion, minced
½ tbs dill
1 cup sour cream

Directions:
Saute onion, green peppers. Add fish and saute until lightly colored. Add in paprika, dill, wine. Put the lid on the pot and simmer until fish is done. Gently fold in the sour cream. Simmer a few more minutes to warm the sour cream.

Mexican Steamed Fish

Mexicans use red snapper, but you can substitute just about any pan fish including white perch, black bass, or walleye.

Ingredients:

4 red snappers, cleaned
1 tbs salt, plus extra to taste
juice of 2 limes
½ cup vegetable oil for frying
½ tsp dried thyme
2 tomatoes, coarsely chopped
½ cup cider vinegar
2 tsp minced chile
½ cup flour
1 medium-size onion, minced
black pepper to taste
3 cups water

Directions:

Wash the fish in a mixture of salted water and vinegar.

Score the fish diagonally from head to tail. Mix the salt and the minced chile pepper together into a paste and place a bit of it into the slits in the fish. Cover the fish with the lime juice and allow it to sit for at least 1 hour.

Remove the fish from the marinade and dry it off. Roll it in the flour and shake off the excess. Heat the oil in a heavy skillet. Place the fish in the oil and fry it over medium heat until golden brown; remove the fish and set it aside. Add the onion, thyme, whole chile, salt and pepper to the oil and cook until the onion is light brown, stirring occasionally. Add the tomatoes and cook until the mixture becomes a thick sauce. Add the water and bring the sauce to a boil. Lower the heat and continue to cook for about 5 minutes. Add the fish and cook for an additional 5 minutes, turning the fish once. Just before removing, add a squeeze of lime juice and stir once. Serve with rice.

Simple Fish in Foil

Just about any fish fillet will do.

Ingredients:

1 lb fish fillets
2 tbs lemon juice
2 potatoes, in ¼ inch strips
1 cup French style green beans
¼ tsp dried dill weed
4 slices onion
2 med carrots, ⅛ inch slices

Directions:

Place each fish fillet in the center of a piece of foil,
12 by 18 inches. Combine dill and lemon juice. Drizzle
over fillets. Top with onion slices. Arrange potatoes
and carrots on sides of fillets. Top with green beans.
Seal foil and put in hot coals of campfire for about 30
minutes or until fork tender.

Streamside Trout

I call this one Streamside Trout because it is so
basic that you can do it along your favorite trout
stream on your camp stove. It is basic, also, because
you don't have to do too much to trout or any fish
when they are that fresh.

Ingredients:

2 whole dressed trout or 4 fillets
½ cup cornmeal
salt and pepper
cooking oil

Directions:

Put salt, pepper and cornmeal in paper bag. Drop
trout in bag and shake vigorously to coat with mixture. Place in hot frying pan and cook until golden
brown.

Trout ala Smith

This recipe came from Arizona college professor Norm Smith who uses it on any trout he outsmarts.

Ingredients:
2 whole trout, dressed
4 slices onion
2 tsp margarine
2 strips bacon
salt and pepper

Directions:
Salt and pepper the inside of each trout, place the onion inside the cavity and place the butter on the trout. Double wrap the fish in foil and put it directly on the coals for about 5 to 7 minutes (depending on the size of the trout), turn them over for the same period. It is best not to have more than a couple of trout per foil package.

GAME

Squirrel Pot Pie

Ingredients:
2 squirrels
2 slices salt pork
1 tsp salt
1 onion
1½ cup coarse dry bread crumbs
Marinade (recipe below)
2 tbs flour
½ tsp black pepper
1 tsp cornstarch

MARINADE:
For game meats such as mature deer or antelope.

for commercial meats such as lamb. Also for small game, upland birds.

Ingredients:
½ **cup peanut oil**
½ **cup brandy**
1 **crumbled bay leaf**
1 **cup dry vermouth**
3 **tbs fresh lemon juice**
2 **cup cool water**

Directions:
Mix the liquids for the marinade thoroughly. It is best done at home ahead of time with the kitchen blender. Add bay leaf. Stir this marinade often as it is being used as it tends to separate.

Cut squirrels into serving sized pieces and marinate 1 to 1½ hours. Drain and blot dry. Chop salt pork coarsely and saute it in skillet until it begins to brown. Mix flour, salt and pepper and dredge meat in mixture, coating each piece thoroughly. Brown meat in skillet with the bacon. Pour hot water over the meat, covering it completely. Cover and simmer over slow heat 45 minutes or until tender. Remove meat to a hot platter, draining pan juices back into skillet.

Bring liquid to a boil. Chop onions to a fine dice or grate it and add to pan liquids. Cook 5 minutes until onion is tender. Test and adjust seasonings. Add cornstarch to cold water and stir into a thin paste. Blend it into the liquid or blend flour and butter into smooth paste and flake into pan, stirring to a smooth gravy. Return the pieces of meat to the pan for a few minutes. Remove from heat, and sprinkle a thick coating of dry bread crumbs over the top.

Venison Stew

Ingredients:

1 lb venison, one-inch cubes
1 tsp lemon juice
1 clove garlic, minced
salt to taste
3 carrots, quartered
3 potatoes, in ½ inch cubes
2 cups hot water
1 tsp worcestershire sauce
1 medium onions, sliced
1 tsp sugar
4 small whole onions
¼ lb margarine

Directions:

Brown meat thoroughly in margarine in large heavy kettle. Add all ingredients, except carrots, whole onions and potatoes. Simmer for 2 hours, adding water if necessary. Add carrots, whole onions and potatoes and cook about 30 minutes. Liquid may be thickened with flour if desired.

Three Minute Venison Steak

If you don't like blood rare steak, don't try this one. You can cook the venison longer, but the longer you cook it the less taste it has and the tougher the meat gets.

Ingredients:

4 venison steaks, ½ inch thick
¼ lb margarine
salt and pepper

Directions:

Heat margarine until smoking hot. Put steaks in skillet, sprinkle with salt and pepper. After 1½ minutes, flip steaks and salt and pepper other side. Remove from heat and serve after 1½ minutes. They will be bloody rare, but good.

Squirrel Stew

Ingredients:
2 squirrels, disjointed
6 oz can corn
2 slices salt pork, diced
3 potatoes, diced
2 pt canned tomatoes
3 onions, diced
½ lb lima beans
1 stalk celery, diced
salt and pepper to taste
¼ cup worcestershire sauce
flour

Directions:
Place the squirrels in a large kettle with enough water to half cover and bring to a boil. Put lid on the kettle. Simmer until squirrels are tender and cool. Remove squirrels from stock and remove meat from bones. Place squirrels back in stock and add remaining ingredients except flour. Cook for 2 hours. Thicken with small amount of flour mixed with water and simmer for 30 minutes longer.

Braised Rabbit with Gravy

Ingredients:
1 rabbit, in pieces
3 tbs cooking fat or oil
2 cups milk
flour, salt, pepper
¼ cup hot water
2 tbs flour

Directions:
Roll rabbit in mixture of flour, salt, and pepper. Heat fat or oil in a heavy fry pan and brown the rabbit slowly, turning to brown on all sides. Add water and cover pan tightly.

Reduce heat and cook slowly until meat is tender (about 1 hour), adding a little more water if needed. Uncover and cook 5 minutes longer to recrisp surface. Remove rabbit from pan and keep it hot. Remove fat from pan and pour back 2 tablespoonfuls. Stir in the 2 tablespoons flour and cook until mixture bubbles. Add milk slowly, stirring constantly. Cook until thick, stirring occasionally, then cook a little longer. Add salt and pepper if needed. To braise a large rabbit (about 4 pounds), use 1/3 cup fat or oil for browning and 1/3 cup water. Cook about 1½ hours, or until tender. Make gravy with 3 tablespoons flour, 3 tablespoons fat, and 3 cups milk.

Rabbit Brunswick Stew

Brunswick stew was one of the basic meals of the frontier homes.

Ingredients:
2 cooking oil
1 onion, chopped
1 can (16 oz) whole kernel corn
2 tsp salt
3 cups of water

2 young rabbits, cut in pieces
1 cup bread crumbs
1 can (16 oz) lima beans
dash pepper

Directions:

In pot, heat the oil and brown pieces of rabbit on all sides. Remove rabbit. Add onion in Dutch oven and cook 3 minutes. Return rabbit and add water, bread crumbs and vegetables, salt and pepper. Bring pot to boil, cover and simmer over low heat for about 35 minutes. Note: For older rabbits, which tend to be tough, parboil* them in salted water and then proceed with recipe.

*Cook until partially done before beginning

Curried Goose Breast

Any goose breasts will do.

Ingredients:
2 goose breasts cut in pieces
2 tbs cooking oil
1 cut onions diced
1 cup chicken stock
1 tbs curry powder
4 tbs flour
1 cub celery diced
½ green pepper diced
dash paprika

Directions:

Put flour in paper bag. Shake pieces of goose breast in bag and fry in frying pan that has a lid. When meat is browned, remove from pan. Put celery, onions and pepper in pan and saute over low heat until soft. Return goose to pan and add chicken stock, curry powder and paprika. Bring pan to boil and then reduce heat to simmer or low, cover and cook for 20 minutes. Remove lid and if gravy is watery add a little more flour from bag. Cook for five more minutes and serve over rice.

Skillet Grouse Dinner

With the required preparation, a delicious grouse dinner can be thrown together in ten minutes. It is ideal for the camp cook who has been out all day stumping the fields in search of game. If you don't have grouse, four to six quail, or six doves can be substituted.

Ingredients:
picked meat 2 ruffed grouse
1 can of mixed vegetables
1 onion, sliced
1 tomato, cut in wedges
1 small can tomato puree
2 cups diced potatoes, cooked
2 tbs cooking oil
1 green peppers, cut in strips
1 can gravy

Directions:
Cook grouse ahead of time by boiling in lightly salted water for ½ hour. Heat oil in skillet and lightly saute onion slices and pepper strips. Add meat and vegetables and heat through. Combine gravy and puree and add to mixture. Season with salt and pepper to taste. Bring to boil, stir. Cook six minutes.

Preparation of Catch

FILLETING A FISH

Most fish don't have to be cleaned or even scaled for filleting. However, for some species like the largemouth bass or grouper it may be desirable to cut away the skin for optimum flavor.

With a firm hold on the head of the fish, make an initial cut as pictured. **Do not cut through the backbone.**

Hold the fillet section and carefully cut away from the rib section and through the stomach skin to free the fillet. Turn fish and repeat procedure on the other side.

Avoid cutting into the rib cage as you run your knife the length of the backbone and cut through the skin just above the tail.

To remove skin, lay fillet with skin side down. Hold the tail firmly while cutting between meat and skin and length of the fillet—starting just forward of tail.

CLEANING A FISH

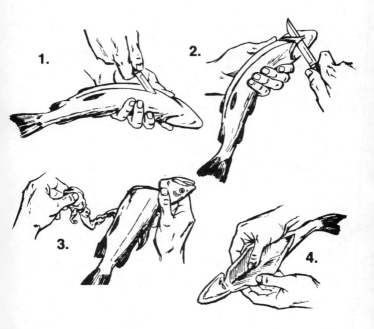

Hold the fish, belly up, in the palm of the hand with your thumb and forefinger in the gills to secure a good grip. 1) Slit the skin open from the vent (near the tail) to the gills. 2) Make a cross-cut at the head to separate the lower junction of the gills from the skin. 3) While holding the gills firmly, pull the fish backward to release the gills and other internal organs. Be sure to clean out the body cavity thoroughly. 4) Along the backbone, you'll see a black streak covered by a membrane. Cut this membrane by scratching the length of the backbone with a knife, and push out the black material with your thumb. Check again to make sure the fish is cleaned thoroughly. Scale the fish if you wish, wipe it dry, and store it in a cool place until you're ready to cook it.

PLANNING INDEX

In some respects, this may be the most important section in this cookbook. Careful planning can make or break a trip into the outdoors, and that is what this index is all about.

There is nothing worse than a camp cook who runs out of cooking fuel. Be careful to have enough fuel for the recipes you select. To assist you in this task, we have arranged the recipes in this index by main ingredient and total prep and cooking time, with the shortest cooking times first. Prep and cooking times are shown in the two columns.

At the end of each list you will find the recipes that take a great deal of simmering time. These dishes should be reserved for camp situations where a stove is available that can hold a great deal of fuel.

Obviously, it makes sense to limit the amount of gear you take with you, no matter what your transportation. For this reason, most of the recipes are one-pot or stir fry meals. One-pot meals are indicated with a * and stir fry recipes with a •.

m = minutes   hr = hours

BEEF	PREP TIME	COOKING TIME	
* Meal in a Fry Pan	5m	15m	..... **47**
* One-Pot Ground Beef Meals	5m	15m	..... **46**
* Easy-Skillet Supper	7m	15m	..... **44**
* Same Old Stuff (SOS)	5m	23m	..... **24**
* Southwest Beef & Rice	10m	20m	..... **45**
* Western Skillet Stew	5m	25m	..... **45**
• Crunchy Bean Sprouts with Beef	13m	17m	..... **42**
* Earl's Hurry Up Chili	5m	25m	..... **48**
* Macaroni Skillet Supper	10m	20m	..... **56**
Beef Easy Supper Dish	10m	25m	..... **56**
* Carne Gisada con Papas	10m	25m	..... **40**
* Mountain Man Beef Stew	10m	30m	..... **55**
• Beef and Broccoli with Garlic Sauce	30m	7m	..... **43**
Black Bean Chili with Rice	10m	30m	..... **30**
* Stuffed Peppers	35m	25m	..... **38**
Rinderrouladen	10m	55m	..... **29**
* Old Settlers Stew	10m	60m	..... **54**
* Beef and Tequila Stew	10m	1 hr 10m	..... **40**
Beef Tips on Rice	7m	1 hr 30m	..... **44**
* Cajun Style Chili	10m	1 hr 30m	..... **47**